TALES OF THE DEAD

ANCIENT ROME

Written by Stewart Ross
Consultant Dr. Hugh Bowden
Illustrated by Inklink & Richard Bonson

DK

LONDON, NEW YORK, MUNICH,
MELBOURNE AND DELHI

EDITOR Kate Simkins
ART EDITOR/STORY VISUALIZER John Kelly
ART DIRECTOR Mark Richards
PUBLISHING MANAGER Simon Beecroft
PUBLISHER Alex Allan
PRODUCTION Erica Rosen
DTP DESIGNER Lauren Egan

First American Edition, 2005

Published in the United States by
DK Publishing, Inc.
375 Hudson Street
New York, New York 10014

05 06 07 08 09   10 9 8 7 6 5 4 3 2

A Cataloging-in-Publication record for this book is available from the Library of Congress.

ISBN 0-7566-1147-4

Color reproduction by Colourscan, Singapore
Printed and bound in China by Leo Paper Products

Discover more at
www.dk.com

ACKNOWLEDGMENTS

Richard Bonson painted the fort (pages 6–7), villa (pages 16–17), street scene (pages 20–21) and Colosseum (pages 28–29).

Inklink painted all other artworks, including the graphic novel.

CONTENTS

CONTINUED FROM PREVIOUS PAGE →

1 FOOD STORE

Massive granaries held enough wheat to last the winter. If the fort was attacked, soldiers could avoid being starved into surrender. The floor was raised off the ground to keep the wheat cool.

2 NERVE CENTER

At the center of the fort stood the headquarters, or *principia*. On ceremonial occasions, soldiers paraded in the main hall of the headquarters. The *principia* also contained a special room that housed the army's standards (*see page 8*).

3 LIVING IN STYLE

The fort commander lived in a large villa next to the headquarters. His family lived with him, along with their many slaves. The commander often ate delicious meals of specially imported meats, served with fine Italian wines not available to the ordinary troops.

12 HOT SOAK

Soldiers cleaned themselves in the bathhouse. They went through a series of hot, steamy rooms, then soaked in a warm bath. They finished with a cold bath.

9 BARRACKS

Soldiers were housed in long buildings called barracks. A century of soldiers (a unit of 80 men) lived in ten blocks along the barracks. Each block had two rooms: a sleeping room with eight bunk beds and a storage room for equipment.

10 CENTURION'S QUARTERS

Each century of soldiers was commanded by a centurion. He lived in his own private apartment at one end of the barracks.

11 PUBLIC RESTROOM

Soldiers had no privacy in the toilets. Wooden seats were placed over a stone channel that allowed the waste to flow out. Instead of toilet paper, soldiers used sponges on sticks!

MY TIME SOLDIERING FOR ROME IS OVER...

...AS, I BELIEVE, IS YOURS, HORTALUS?

YES, I'M RETURNING TO ROME AT ONCE.

ROMAN ATTACKS ON REBEL TRIBES ARE GETTING HARSHER.

THE EMPEROR WANTS ALL RESISTANCE CRUSHED...

...VILLAGE BY VILLAGE!

YOUR FAMILY IS NEARBY, ISN'T IT, JUBA?

YES, MY CHILDREN, SABINA AND PUBLIUS.

"WELL, I WARN YOU, JUBA...

...AS A FRIEND...

...GET THEM OUT OF HERE - FAST!"

MAY THE GODS PROTECT US!

I MUST GO TO MY CHILDREN!

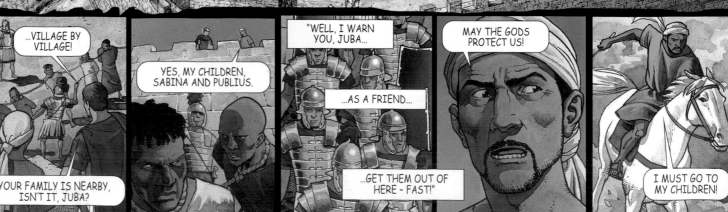

4 A SOLDIER'S DUTIES

Soldiers didn't just fight. They also went on guard duty, policed the nearby towns, tended to the fort's horses, and washed clothes and bedding. One of the worst jobs must have been cleaning the toilets, which often became blocked!

FRONTIER FORT

STORY CONTINUES ON NEXT PAGE

The Romans built huge, fortified camps along their frontiers. The job of the soldiers who lived in the forts was to keep invaders out and uphold law and order among local populations. Forts were made of stone, brick, wood, and earth. They were like small towns. Some covered up to 54 acres (22 hectares), larger than 40 football fields! Inside, the soldiers had everything they needed—housing, food supplies, workshops, stables, offices, baths, and a medical center.

"ROME WILL PROTECT US!"

5 GOING TO TOWN

Towns grew up around the forts. Here, traders encouraged soldiers to spend their pay on goods and services, including food and wine. Some soldiers secretly married local women.

LISTEN, CHILDREN! I'VE BEEN MADE A ROMAN CITIZEN.

7 TENDING TO THE SICK

Wounded soldiers were cared for in the hospital. Doctors cleaned and bandaged wounds. With so many soldiers living in cramped quarters, disease was common.

"WE HAVE VERY LITTLE TIME!"

6 GATE DEFENSES

After a patrol's regular tour of the surrounding area, it marches through the fort's main gate. Most forts had four gates, each defended by heavily guarded towers.

...TO DESTROY THE VILLAGE!

8 WALLED IN

The stone walls were up to 6½ feet (2 meters) thick and reinforced with a bank of earth. They were surrounded by a deep ditch and were extremely difficult to knock down.

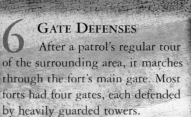

LET ME THROUGH! EMERGENCY!

IT'S FATHER!

RACE YOU TO HIM!

FORGET IT, SLOWPOKE!

THE ROMANS ARE COMING...

CONTINUED FROM PREVIOUS PAGE

NO BARBARIAN REBELS MUST ESCAPE...

...ORDERS ARE ORDERS...

P-P-PLEASE SIR...

...OUR FATHER IS JUBA, A ROMAN CITIZEN.

MANY PEOPLES, ONE EMPIRE

The greatest Roman achievement was creating an empire from many different cultures. They managed this by making membership of the Empire desirable— people were generally safer and better off under Roman rule than outside it. Territories under Roman rule were called provinces.

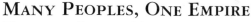

BRITONS
The Romans conquered southern Britain (Britannia) in the first century CE. They built Hadrian's Wall to keep out the Scots.

GERMANS
Only a few of the tribes of Germani (Germans) were absorbed into the Roman Empire. Their frontier with Rome was often at the center of fierce fighting.

DACIANS
Dacia (modern Romania) was conquered by Emperor Trajan in 106 CE. The victory was commemorated in carvings on Trajan's column in Rome.

GAULS
The Gauls lived in what is now France, Belgium, Switzerland, Austria, and northern Italy. These Celtic lands were taken into the Roman Empire over many years.

ROMANS
The tribes of central Italy were the first Romans. As they conquered lands and people, they spread their way of life over a vast area.

SPANIARDS
Spain, then called Hispania, became part of the Roman Empire over many years. Many senators, writers, and orators came from Spain, as did the Emperor Trajan.

Rome

MAURETANIANS
Sabina and Publius were from Mauretania. Although many local people resisted Roman rule, some, like Juba, became auxiliary soldiers in the Roman army.

NUMIDIANS
Numidia was part of the Roman province of Africa. The name comes from the Latin for "nomads" (people with no fixed home).

SO WHAT?

YOU'LL JOIN THE OTHER PRISONERS!

OW!

WHILE OUR VILLAGE WAS BURNED TO THE GROUND...

...WE WERE TIED...

...AND LED AWAY.

SENATOR
A few hundred senators ruled Rome. These wealthy men were mostly from the nobility (upper classes).

EQUESTRIAN
Equestrians made up the second tier of Roman society. They were often army officers.

FREE BORN
Most of the Romans were ordinary citizens. They could be rich, poor, or middle-class.

FREED SLAVE
A slave who had been given his freedom became a citizen. Some freed slaves were rich.

SLAVES
Slaves were owned by Roman citizens or the Empire. They did all the hard work for no pay.

ROMAN SOCIETY
The people living in the Roman Empire were either citizens, foreigners, or slaves. Citizens were of Roman descent. Some foreigners could become citizens after serving in the Roman army. Slaves were not citizens and had no rights at all.

PARTHIANS
The Parthians lived in what is now Iran. They fought many wars with the Romans but were never conquered by them.

EGYPTIANS
Egypt, the home of the greatest early civilization, was a source of wonder to the Romans. The first emperor, Augustus, took over Egypt in 31 BCE.

ROMAN TRADE
Although the Roman Empire was conquered by soldiers, trade was important for holding it together. The Empire allowed merchants to buy and sell goods over a huge area. This helped make the inhabitants of the Roman world much better off than those living beyond its frontiers.

CLOTH
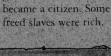
The Romans made cloth from wool and flax, but luxurious silk came overland all the way from China.

ANIMALS AND GRAIN
Thousands of exotic wild animals were imported from Africa. Grain came from many parts of the Empire.

HORSES AND OIL
Some of the best horses came from North Africa. Olive oil was produced in Italy but also imported from other areas.

WINE
By Juba's time, wine from southern Gaul was being exported all over the Roman world.

THE ROMAN WORLD
The Roman Empire included many nations and races who shared a way of life. The first Romans came from Rome and then from the region that is now Italy. In the later Empire, the Romans allowed a wide range of different peoples to call themselves Romans. They spoke the same language (Latin), obeyed the same laws, and used the same money. They were all ruled by the Emperor, who was not necessarily of Italian birth.

...LYING DEAD ON A BATTLEFIELD.

...AND OF FATHER...

ALL I COULD THINK OF WAS FATHER.

WE WERE MARCHED TO THE PORT OF HIPPO...

...AND LOADED ONTO A SHIP...

...WITH OTHER PRISONERS OF WAR.

ALL WE HAD NOW WERE TEARS...

...AND MEMORIES OF HOME...

2 STABLE MATES
In the stables, a team of grooms and stable lads cared for the household's many horses. There was always a blacksmith, who made the horseshoes.

3 STOREROOMS
The Romans did not have refrigeration, so food had to be dried or smoked before it was stored. It was important to have the storerooms full before winter, when there was little fresh food available.

1 FARM WORK
As the last of the wheat was harvested with scythes, an ox-drawn plow prepared the soil for next year's crop.

9 THE KITCHEN
The kitchen was like a restaurant kitchen, producing meals for dozens of people. Most cooking was done over an open fire, although bread and cakes were baked in circular ovens.

WE WERE REALLY LONELY AT FIRST.

THEY WORKED US HARD...

...PUBLIUS AS A STABLE LAD...

STEADY, GIRL!

...AND ME AS A HOUSEMAID.

FETCH WATER FOR THE KITCHENS, SABINA!

ROMAN VILLA

A villa was a large country house built around a courtyard. There were two basic types of villas: farm and luxury. Most, like the one here, were at the heart of a farming estate. Luxury villas were built by the very wealthy as places for relaxation. The emperors, for instance, had elegant seaside villas where they went in the summer to escape the heat. The finest villas had baths, gardens, drains, elegant decoration, running water, and (in cold climates) underfloor heating.

BY DAY, WE WERE TOO BUSY TO THINK ABOUT HOME...

...AND WE SOON GOT USED TO THE ROUTINE.

HNNNNFFFF!

DRUSILLA WAS KIND, AND WE HAD ENOUGH TO EAT.

RACE YOU TO THE MILESTONE!

WE JUST HAD TO KEEP OUT OF THE WAY OF THE OWNER'S ROWDY SONS.

PUBLIUS AND I LOOKED OUT FOR EACH OTHER.

ARE YOU OK, PUBLIUS?

4 KITCHEN GARDEN

The villa's supply of fruit, vegetables, herbs, and spices came from its own kitchen garden. Nearby beehives provided honey for sweetening food.

5 WATER SUPPLY

Water was brought to the biggest villas in special pipes and channels. This villa has a large pool. Slaves collected all the water needed for cooking, drinking, and washing from here in buckets.

6 FORMAL GARDEN

The formal garden was laid out in a neat design. Along one side ran a shady walkway (colonnade) in which the family could exercise without getting wet or sunburned.

7 THE ATRIUM

The heart of the villa was the atrium, which was a room for meeting guests and a living room. It was decorated with mosaics and often had a pool for collecting rainwater.

8 BEDROOM SPACE

A Roman bedroom was much emptier than a modern one. Clothes and bedding were stored in a wooden chest. Only the villa's owner and his family had the luxury of wooden beds.

I WON'T BE STAYING LONG...
...BUT I INTEND TO INSPECT THE RUNNING OF MY VILLA.

THERE ARE NEW SLAVES?
YES, MASTER. A BOY AND A GIRL.

WELCOME BACK, MASTER.
DRUSILLA!

A HORSEMAN...
...WHO IS IT?

BUT AT NIGHT...

...WE STILL MISSED FATHER TERRIBLY.

HAVE YOU SEEN ANY PRISONERS OF WAR FROM AFRICA?
NO, SORRY! TRY THE ROAD TO ROME.

YES, I'VE SEEN THEM...

...HEADING FOR ROME!

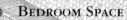

CONTINUED FROM PREVIOUS PAGE →

WE RODE ALL NIGHT.

THEN, JUST AS WE WERE NEARING ROME...

WHAT'S THAT AHEAD?!

WHOA!

LOOK OUT! RUNAWAY HORSE!

1 MAKING BREAD

Bread was the basic food of most Romans. The dough was cooked in big, round ovens.

2 WINERY

Watered-down wine, made from grape juice, was the Romans' favorite drink. The press in the middle of the room is for squashing juice out of grapes.

10 GRAFFITI

If the Romans found a blank wall, they scribbled on it! The city of Pompeii, for instance, had over 3,500 pieces of graffiti.

9 STORE FRONTS

Shops were on the ground floor of houses or apartments. Because they had no glass, they were like market stands. There was no refrigeration, so shoppers had to make sure the food was still fresh.

8 STONE HEROES

Statues decorated the main streets and meeting places. Some were religious. Others were of famous soldiers, politicians, speakers, and writers.

PERHAPS WE CAN HELP!

QUICK, AFTER IT!

I THINK WE'RE GAINING!

GRAB THE REINS!

WHOA! STEADY! IT'S ALL RIGHT!!

WELL DONE, YOU TWO!

THIS NEW HORSE IS FAST BUT A LITTLE WILD!

WE'RE FROM THE BLUES CHARIOT-RACING TEAM.

WHERE ARE YOU HEADING?

LIVING IN ROME

3 BUILDING UP
An apartment building or *insula* is under construction. Workers cover the roof with clay tiles and plaster the walls. Most town-dwellers lived in apartments like this one.

Rome was a thrilling city! With a population of around one million, it was by far the largest city in the Roman Empire. Some of it looked very grand, with elegant temples and beautiful statues. Its thousands of shops, market stands, and restaurants sold everything one could wish for, from hot food to the finest jewelry. But Rome was also dirty and overcrowded, with poor people living in tiny rooms. Traffic jams often blocked the streets, and thieves preyed on unwary citizens.

4 CLEAN CLOTHES
The people on the top floor of this apartment are doing the laundry. Women are hanging the clothes out to dry in the sun. The woman in blue is weaving material on a loom.

5 BIG FANS
Cheered on by its supporters, a chariot-racing team parades through the streets. Roman race fans were as passionate about their team as football fans are today. Go, Reds!

6 ANIMAL HOMES
Domestic animals, such as cows, pigs, and chickens, were kept in city gardens—and even inside people's homes. Fortunately, most were better cared for than this unfortunate cow!

7 PUBLIC WATER
Very few homes had their own running water. Public supplies were piped into the city's pools and fountains, from where people carried the water inside in buckets.

ESCAPED, EH?

YOU DON'T DENY IT? RIGHT, HERE'S WHAT I'M GOING TO DO...

HERE THEY ARE, BRUTUS!

MMMMMPHHH!

BUT SUDDENLY...

UH...GOING TO ROME...

...TO LOOK FOR WORK.

WORK? YOU'RE IN LUCK!

COME WITH ME—THE BLUES ALWAYS NEED GOOD STABLE HANDS.

AS WE ENTERED THE CITY...

...EVERYONE BEGAN CHEERING THE BLUES!

WAIT A MINUTE! I RECOGNIZE THOSE TWO SLAVES!

COME ON, BOY!

WE FOLLOWED THE BLUES TO THEIR STABLES.

PLEASING THE GODS

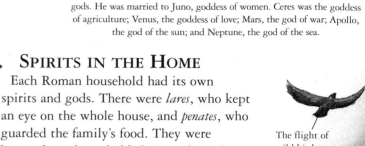

At the time of Sabina and Publius, the Romans believed in many gods and spirits. To keep the gods happy, the Romans made them offerings, such as incense or food, and held ceremonies. People also had to worship the Emperor. Refusing to do so was a serious crime—treason.

The Romans had hundreds of gods and goddesses. Jupiter was king of the gods. He was married to Juno, goddess of women. Ceres was the goddess of agriculture; Venus, the goddess of love; Mars, the god of war; Apollo, the god of the sun; and Neptune, the god of the sea.

Household shrine— the statues represented gods or the spirits of respected ancestors.

SPIRITS IN THE HOME

Each Roman household had its own spirits and gods. There were *lares*, who kept an eye on the whole house, and *penates*, who guarded the family's food. They were honored at a household shrine, where the head of the house—usually the father—led regular worship. The family left an offering, such as bread or wine, or promised the god or goddess something in the hope that their wishes would be granted.

The flight of wild birds was thought to carry messages from the gods.

MAKING SACRIFICES

Animals were killed (sacrificed) to please the gods at an altar outside the temple. During a sacrifice, the words and movements had to be just right— even a dog barking might ruin the whole ceremony. The Romans believed that the greater the value of the animal, the more pleased the gods would be.

Priests were highly trained in making sacrifices. They also read signs from the gods, sometimes by examining the insides of the animals they had sacrificed.

Goat has been killed either to thank the gods or to beg a favor from them.

Animals had to be killed with one well-aimed blow of an ax.

Valuable, fat pig waiting to be sacrificed

Elderly woman soothsayer, believed to be able to see into the future

Left sidebar panels

BRUTUS SOLD US TO A LAUNDRY OWNER.

I WASHED TOGAS, TREADING THEM ALL DAY.

PUBLIUS WORKED BLEACHING CLOTHES.

THE FUMES WERE POISONOUS...

... AND HE OFTEN PASSED OUT.

Bottom panels

THE OVERSEER WAS MERCILESS.

YOU SCUM!

GET UP AND GET BACK TO WORK!

BUT OUR NEW OWNER DIDN'T LIKE CRUELTY...

...AND OFTEN GOT ANGRY WITH THE OVERSEER.

WE SLEPT AT THE LAUNDRY.

IT WAS OUR ONLY CHANCE TO TALK.

THEN, ONE NIGHT...

IT'S THE OVERSEER!

CHRISTIANITY TAKES OVER

At first the Romans mostly ignored Christianity, a religion that began in and around Judea (modern-day Israel and Palestine) in about 30 CE. By Juba's time, some Christians were being persecuted because they refused to make offerings of incense to the Emperor's statue. But they continued to meet in secret, and their religion spread around the Roman world. Eventually, after 313 BCE, Christianity was adopted by the Emperor and became the major religion of the Empire.

New Christians were welcomed with a ceremony of washing known as baptism.

CULT OF ISIS
The Egyptian goddess Isis was worshiped all over the Empire.

JUDAISM
Unlike the Romans, the Jews believed in one all-powerful god.

MITHRAS
Mithras, the Persian sun god famous for killing a ferocious bull, was popular with Roman soldiers serving along the frontiers.

MIXED-UP GODS

As the Empire spread, non-Roman gods and goddesses were adopted by the Romans The British goddess Sul, for example, was merged with the Roman Minerva, the goddess of arts and crafts. Similarly, the Greek Zeus, king of the gods, was combined with Jupiter.

VESTAL VIRGINS

The four or six Vestal Virgins were chosen from Rome's best families. They were not allowed to marry and had to serve for 30 years in the temple of Vesta, the goddess of the fireplace. Their most important job was keeping alight the sacred temple flame. The Romans believed that if the flame went out, disaster would strike Rome.

The temple, built on sacred ground, housed statues of gods but was not a place of worship.

Architecture in Greek style, with massive columns, was the favorite temple design.

Emperors were worshiped as gods during their lifetime and after their death.

The Vestal Virgins left home to join the temple of Vesta before they were ten years old.

Procession headed by a worshiper carrying a picture of the god or goddess being honored

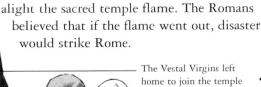

THE OVERSEER HAD GOTTEN HIS REVENGE!

BUT...WHAT FOR?

TREASON!

YOUR OVERSEER INFORMS US THAT YOU REFUSE TO PRAY TO THE EMPEROR.

BUT LATER, HE RETURNED WITH THE GUARDS.

YOU'RE UNDER ARREST!

OVERSEER, I TRUSTED YOU...

...LEAVE AND NEVER COME BACK!

HE'S A THIEF!

THE NEXT MORNING, THE OVERSEER BLAMED ME.

BUT IT WASN'T ME, MASTER!

NO! IT WAS HIM! HE'S THE THIEF!

LOOK!

CONTINUED FROM PREVIOUS PAGE ➔

Ladies' jewelry

RICH AND POOR

Life as a Roman very much depended on money and position in society. Rich nobles enjoyed all kinds of privileges, including top jobs and luxurious homes. The very poor had to make a living any way they could, often by begging or stealing. In between were the majority of Romans, who could be anything from wealthy merchants to shopkeepers or potters. But the Empire was a place of opportunity, where even freed slaves and foreigners could make their fortunes.

HOW DO I LOOK?

Rich Roman ladies usually wore makeup. They powdered their faces with chalk and lined their eyes with ash. Elaborate hairstyles and wigs were fashionable. Most Romans were naturally dark-haired, so wigs made from the blond hair of prisoners of war were popular.

TOGA PARTY!

The Romans loved a good party. Those with money to spare held lavish banquets of rich food and spectacular amusements. Guests ate with their fingers or with spoons, and the meal could go on for several hours. Some parties were serious and intellectual, with poetry-reading and speeches. The wilder ones, where the red wine flowed freely, sometimes ended up as drunken riots.

Slave musicians play horns, pipes, a tambourine, and a lyre.

Dancing slave girls

Guests reclined on couches and ate from low tables.

Slaves carry in a stuffed swan.

Poet entertains the guests.

Hosts showed off by providing lavish dishes and many courses.

Comic strip (left column):

MEANWHILE...

ROME AT LAST!

NOW TO THE SLAVE MARKETS.

I'M LOOKING FOR THE SLAVE DEALER BRUTUS.

I'VE BEEN TOLD HE KNOWS WHERE MY CHILDREN ARE.

YOU'LL FIND HIM AT THE BATHS MOST MORNINGS.

Comic strip (bottom row):

BRUTUS, THE SLAVE DEALER?

WHO ARE YOU?

I AM JUBA, A ROMAN CITIZEN FROM MAURETANIA. I BELIEVE YOU SOLD MY CHILDREN...

...AS SLAVES!

I DON'T KNOW WHAT YOU'RE TALKING ABOUT.

NOW, GET LOST!

I WARN YOU, BRUTUS— I HAVE POWERFUL FRIENDS.

STORY CONTINUES ON NEXT PAGE →

Shop selling wine

Carts could hardly get through the narrow streets.

People bought hot food from carry-out counters.

Children begging were a common sight.

IN THE BACK STREETS

The garbage-strewn back streets of Rome crawled with dirt, disease, and cruelty. Muggers lurked in dark corners. Beggars grabbed at passers-by. Shopkeepers and street vendors cried their wares, while carts, donkeys, pedestrians, and stray dogs jostled together in the crowded roadway. From time to time, plague swept through the city, killing thousands. Not surprisingly, few poor people lived beyond the age of 40.

WHAT ROMANS ATE

Bread was the basic food of most Romans. What went with it depended on wealth—the poor might be able to afford vegetables, eggs, or a piece of sausage. The better-off also enjoyed a wide range of fruits, fish, and meat. Most food was freshly prepared, making the Roman diet a healthy one. Only the rich had their own kitchens and ate at home. Ordinary Romans bought hot or cold snacks from carry-out counters or ate in cheap restaurants. The main meal was usually in the afternoon.

Wine mixed with water was the most common drink.

Bread was sometimes flavored with cheese or honey.

Cheese was often made from goats' milk.

Fish and shellfish were popular with the well off.

Poultry included chicken and duck.

Meat, such as pork, lamb, and beef, was expensive.

WHERE HE'S GOING!

HE WON'T NEED THEM...

WHAT ABOUT HIS DOCUMENTS?

PUT HIM IN THE CART!

BRUTUS HAS PLANS FOR HIM!

LIKE WHO?

SENATOR HORTALUS!

I SEE... AND HAVE YOU SPOKEN TO HIM ABOUT THIS?

NOT YET, BUT I WILL...

...YOU'LL BE HEARING FROM ME!

HE HAS TO BE STOPPED!

THAT'S HIM!

CRACK!

25

CONTINUED FROM PREVIOUS PAGE

CRIME AND PUNISHMENT

WE WERE BROUGHT BEFORE A MAGISTRATE.

Roman law laid down strict rules that citizens had to obey. Public law was for punishing people who had harmed the state, such as traitors. Punishments were often harsh to discourage other wrongdoers. Private law dealt with disputes between individuals, and cases were normally settled with fines. Some crimes were tried by a judge and a jury of up to 75 citizens. Other crimes were dealt with by officials called magistrates.

Under Roman law, parents were allowed to kill or abandon unwanted children. Others sometimes took these babies, often bringing them up as slaves.

OUR OWNER, A CHRISTIAN, WAS SENTENCED TO DEATH FOR TREASON...

OFF WITH HIS HEAD!

Death was the harshest punishment for an offense against Rome. The accused were often tortured first to make them admit their guilt. There were several gruesome ways of carrying out the death sentence, including burning, drowning in a sack, and crucifixion (*see* page 15). Guilty soldiers were killed quickly by beheading because they had served the state. This was considered a merciful death. Nobles were usually allowed to commit suicide rather than face public execution, while the poor received the worst treatment of all.

...AND WE SLAVES WERE SENT TO...

Condemned soldiers were beheaded with a large sword.

...THE COLOSSEUM...

...TO BE ARENA SLAVES—THE WORST JOB IN ROME!

AFTER THE KILLING...

...WE CLEANED UP.

HURRY UP! THE PRISONERS ARE ON NEXT!

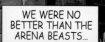

WE WERE NO BETTER THAN THE ARENA BEASTS...

...WAITING FOR DEATH.

SPEAKING UP

Public speaking (oratory) was vital in lawmaking and in the law courts. No one was better at speaking in public than Marcus Tullius Cicero (106–43 BCE). He was a brilliant lawyer who often successfully defended the accused in court with his arguments. Cicero also introduced ideas from ancient Greece into Rome, and his style of speaking influenced many later orators.

Statue of the famous orator Cicero

THROWN TO THE LIONS

One of the cruelest ways the Romans executed criminals was by unleashing wild animals on them at the public games. The animals were starved so they would be sure to pounce on their live meal and tear it apart. Such executions gave a terrifying warning to anyone thinking of committing a crime—and provided grisly entertainment at the same time. Christians who had committed the crime of treason by not worshiping the Emperor were sometimes killed in this way.

Execution beasts included lions, tigers, hyenas, and panthers.

GO TO JAIL!

The lowest level of Rome's state prison was reached only through a narrow trapdoor. The dark, damp cell was used for holding enemies of Rome and for nonpublic executions. The word "incarcerate," meaning "imprison," comes from the name of Rome's prison, the Carcer.

Wooden carved eagle, the symbol of Rome

FATHER!?!!

THEN, AMONG THE CONDEMNED WE SAW...

IT'S THE PRISONERS FOR EXECUTION!
POOR WRETCHES!

IF ONLY FATHER WERE ALIVE...
...TO SAVE US!

YOU'LL NEVER GET AWAY WITH THIS, BRUTUS!

MAKE SURE HE'S ON THE MIDDAY EXECUTION LIST!

YOU CAN'T! I'M A ROMAN CITIZEN!

AND I'M JULIUS CAESAR!

ENJOY THE SHOW!

HOW CAN FATHER HAVE BEEN CONDEMNED TO DEATH?

WE MUST HELP H...

SHHHH! WE'VE GOT TO THINK—FAST!

WE NEED A DIVERSION!

I'LL SAVE HIM!

NO! I HAVE AN IDEA...

1 EXOTIC BEASTS
Animals slaughtered in the arena included elephants, lions, tigers, monkeys, bears, leopards, hippopotamuses, rhinoceroses, giraffes, camels, ostriches, wild boars, wolves, and crocodiles.

2 BIG CROWDS
Spectators sat in rows in steep tiers. They were protected from the sun by a gigantic canvas awning. Suspended from 240 masts, it was operated by 1,000 sailors.

3 RISING PROPS
Scenery, like these palm trees, was raised up from below floor level on huge ramps operated by machinery.

12 WAY IN
There were 80 entrances: 76 for the general public, one for the city magistrates, one for the emperor, and two for the performers.

11 FOUNDATION
The Colosseum was built on marshy ground, so about 327,000 cubic yards (250,000 cubic meters) of concrete had to be laid below ground level to make a solid foundation.

10 UNDERGROUND
The rooms under the arena floor were used for storing scenery, weapons, armor, and even (temporarily) the dead bodies of humans and animals.

9 BRICK AND STONE
One million clay bricks and 131,000 cubic yards (100,000 cubic meters) of stone, cut into blocks and held together with iron clamps, were used to build the arena.

READY?...PULL!

COME ON!

IT'S MOVING!!

WE HAD OPENED THE LIONS' CAGE...

HIYAA!

HIYAA!

WHAT...?!!!

LOOK OUT!

AARGHHH!

STORY CONTINUES ON NEXT PAGE

THE COLOSSEUM

4 EMPEROR'S BOX
The emperor, his family, and guests had their own entrance to a private box beneath a colorful sun shade.

The Amphitheatrum Flavium, known today as the Colosseum, was the grandest amphitheater in the Roman world. Begun by the Emperor Vespasian in 70 CE, it took more than ten years to build. Later emperors altered and improved it. The oval-shaped building seated around 50,000 spectators. Its floor rested on a network of underground rooms and passages that were linked to the arena by trapdoors.

5 BATHROOM BREAK
With such big crowds, the building had to have lots of toilets! They were supplied with water from a system of lead pipes. Another system took away the waste.

6 BEAST VS. BEAST
Animals were forced to fight each other—enraged bulls might fight elephants, for example. Gladiators also fought fierce animals.

8 FLOODING
Since the underground rooms were not there when the Colosseum was first built, it is possible that the arena may have been filled with water. There would have been special games held on the artificial lake.

7 BIG GAME HUNT
Hunters all over the Empire worked to keep the Colosseum supplied with wild animals for its shows. Many thousands of creatures were captured and killed for the amusement of the Romans.

...TO FACE THE MOST POWERFUL MAN IN THE WORLD!

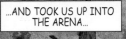
...AND TOOK US UP INTO THE ARENA...

THE GUARDS SEIZED US, TOO...

GET OFF!

RUN, CHILDREN, RUN!

PUBLIUS RUSHED IN TO TRY TO SAVE FATHER.

PUBLIUS?!!

OH, MY SON! MY SON!

WE THOUGHT OUR PLAN HAD WORKED...

...BUT IT WAS TOO LATE...

...MORE GUARDS ARRIVED...

...THEY KILLED THE LIONS...

...AND GRABBED FATHER!

CONTINUED FROM PREVIOUS PAGE

WE THOUGHT WE WOULD DIE A HORRIBLE DEATH.

COURAGE, CHILDREN!

IS THIS PART OF THE GAMES, HORTALUS?

WHAT DO YOU MEAN, SIRE?

OUR FATE WAS IN THE EMPEROR'S HANDS!

PREPARE YOURSELVES FOR DEATH!

SPECTATOR SPORTS

The Romans loved to watch sports, especially violent games. By the reign of Antoninus Pius, there were about 120 official games (*ludi*) a year—around one every three days. Games had once been religious festivals. By this time, they were just free entertainment put on by emperors to please the public. As each emperor tried to outdo his predecessor with more lavish entertainment, putting on games became a major Roman industry.

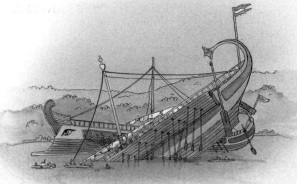

SEA FIGHT
Not many Romans got to see a real live naval battle, so the games' organizers staged their own. They found a suitable lake or made one by flooding an arena. Then real ships and their crews fought sea battles in front of roaring crowds.

There were three chariots for each team, making 12 in each race.

THRILLS AND SPILLS
Chariot racing was the oldest and most popular Roman entertainment. By Sabina and Publius's time, there were four teams: the Blues, Greens, Whites, and Reds. Each was a professional team. Fights between their fans, who bet heavily on the races, were quite common. The light, two-wheeled chariots pulled by four horses raced at breakneck speed around seven circuits of the stadium. Successful charioteers became wealthy superstars, while the less skilled or unlucky were often killed.

Teams were identified by color: Blue, Green, White, or Red.

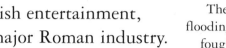

SIRE! I AM A ROMAN CITIZEN!

HOW DARE YOU!

BY THE GODS! IT'S...

...JUBA!

EXCUSE ME, SIRE, BUT HE'S TELLING THE TRUTH!

JUBA, MY FRIEND!

HORTALUS!

HOW DID THIS HAPPEN?

The Retarius gladiator carried a large net and a trident (a forked spear).

The Thracian gladiator fought with a short, curved sword.

A costumed figure with a hammer made sure the dead were really dead.

BLOOD AND SAND

Criminals, slaves, prisoners of war, and even some women had to fight for their lives as gladiators. A few even volunteered. Gladiators were warriors trained for hand-to-hand combat in the sandy arena of an amphitheater. There were rules about who could fight whom. Contests did not always end in death. A gladiator who had an opponent at his or her mercy might ask the crowd whether the defeated fighter should be killed or saved.

Slaves carried away the bodies.

CIRCUS MAXIMUS

Rome's largest chariot-racing stadium was the Circus Maximus, which held an amazing 200,000 people in three massive tiers of seats. The stadium was about 1,800 feet (550 meters) long and 450 feet (137 meters) wide. A full circuit, including tight turns around the posts at each end, was about 4,500 feet (1,370 meters). The center of the Circus was decorated with statues put up by emperors and wealthy citizens.

Chariots often crashed and overturned.

THE END

AT LAST!

...WE WERE TOGETHER AGAIN...

GO, BLUES!

...FATHER WAS MADE THE TEAM'S STABLE MANAGER

WE GOT OUR JOBS BACK WITH THE BLUES...

IT WAS BRUTUS, THE SLAVE DEALER...

LATER...

...BRUTUS PAID FOR HIS CRIME...

...IN THE ARENA.

31

INDEX